W9-BVE-159

It's Valentine's Day

by **Jack Prelutsky**
pictures by **Yossi Abolafia**

Scholastic Inc.
New York Toronto London Auckland Sydney Tokyo

No part of this publication may be reproduced
in whole or in part, or stored in a retrieval
system, or transmitted in any form or by any means,
electronic, mechanical, photocopying, recording,
or otherwise, without written permission of
the publisher. For information regarding permission,
write to William Morrow & Company, Inc.,
105 Madison Avenue, New York, NY 10016.

ISBN 0-590-33585-5

Text copyright © 1983 by Jack Prelutsky.
Illustrations copyright © 1983 by Yossi Abolafia.
All rights reserved.
This edition published by
Scholastic Inc., 730 Broadway, New York, NY 10003,
by arrangement with William Morrow & Company, Inc.

12 11 10 9 8 7 6 5 4 3 2 1   1   5 6 7 8 9/8 0/9

Printed in the U. S. A.   11

FOR CAROLYNN,
MY VALENTYNN
— J.P.

FOR IRIT
— Y.A.

• CONTENTS •

• IT'S VALENTINE'S DAY •

It's Valentine's Day,
and in the street
there's freezing rain,
and slush, and sleet,
the wind is fierce,
the skies are gray,
I don't think I'll
go out today.

But here inside,
the weather's warm,
there is no trace
of wind or storm,
and you just made
the morning shine —
you said you'd be
my valentine.

• A VALENTINE FOR MY TEACHER •

My teacher's very special
so I'm making her a heart,
a valentine that's sure to be
a proper work of art.

I've worked on it all morning
so it should be ready soon,
I'd like to slip it on her desk
before this afternoon.

It's colored in with crayons
and it's trimmed with paper lace,
it has flowers, hearts, and cupids —
I can't *wait* to see her face.

• A VALENTINE FOR MY
BEST FRIEND •

You are rotten, you are crummy,

nasty, smelly, and a dummy,

you are absolutely awful,

and your breath should be unlawful.

You are ugly, you are simple,
and your brain is like a pimple,
you should soak your head in brine....

WON'T YOU BE MY VALENTINE?

Our classroom has a mailbox
that we painted red and gold,
we stuffed it with more valentines
than it was made to hold.

When we opened it this morning

I was nervous as could be,

I wondered if a single one

had been addressed to me.

But when they'd been delivered
I felt twenty stories tall,
I got so many valentines
I couldn't hold them all.

• I MADE MY DOG A VALENTINE •

I made my dog a valentine,
she sniffed it very hard,
then chewed on it a little while
and left it in the yard.

I made one for my parrakeets,
a pretty paper heart,
they pulled it with their claws
and beaks
until it ripped apart.

I made one for my turtle,
all *he* did was get it wet,
I wonder if a valentine
is wasted on a pet.

• I MADE A GIANT VALENTINE •

I made a giant valentine
to mail a special friend,
I'm sorry that I made it
for it's one I'll never send.

This morning at the playground
he was mean and made me sore,
and now I think I'm certain
I don't like him anymore.

He pelted me with snowballs,
seven hit me in the head,
I'm taking home that valentine
to give my cat instead.

• OH NO! •

Oh no!

She kissed me on the cheek,

I'm so mad it's hard to speak,

that's a kiss I *must* erase.

Goodbye!

I'm off to wash my face.

• MY SPECIAL CAKE •

It's Valentine's Day, so I'll create
a special cake to celebrate,
a cake as good as a cake can be
(I'm using my own recipe).

I dump some butter in a bowl,
add licorice as black as coal,
then jellybeans, and eggs, and rice,
and chocolate chips, a touch of spice.

I put in bits of peanut brittle,
salt and sugar (just a little),
flour too (a scoop or so),
and milk to help me mix the dough.

I drop in raisins (half a cup),

then stir and stir and stir it up.

The oven's on, the cake is in,

I'm wiping batter off my chin.

I hope my cake will turn out well....
Wait! What is that awful smell?
It really doesn't look too nice,
I think I'll try a tiny slice.

Yuck! It has an awful taste,

like gluey gobs of smelly paste.

I wonder what I could have done...

I'd better bake another one.

•THERE'S SOMEONE I KNOW•

There's someone I know
whom I simply can't stand,
I wish he would bury
his head in the sand,

or move to the moon
or to deep outer space,
whenever I see him
I make a weird face.

Today during recess
outside in the yard,
he suddenly gave me
a valentine card.

I wish that he hadn't,
it made me upset,
it's the prettiest one
I could possibly get.

• MOTHER'S CHOCOLATE VALENTINE •

I bought a box of chocolate hearts,
a present for my mother,
they looked so good I tasted one,
and then I tried another.

They both were so delicious
that I ate another four,
and then another couple,
and then half a dozen more.

I couldn't seem to stop myself,

I nibbled on and on,

before I knew what happened

all the chocolate hearts were gone.

I felt a little guilty,

I was stuffed down to my socks,

I ate my mother's valentine...

I hope she likes the box.

•I LOVE YOU MORE THAN APPLESAUCE•

I love you more than applesauce,
than peaches and a plum,
than chocolate hearts and cherry tarts
and berry bubblegum.

I love you more than lemonade
and seven-layer cakes,
than lollipops and candy drops
and thick vanilla shakes.

I love you more than marzipan,

than marmalade on toast,

oh I love pies of any size,

but I love YOU the most.

• JELLY JILL LOVES WEASEL WILL •

Jelly Jill loves Weasel Will
and Will loves Flo the Fink,
Flo loves Tom Tomatoface
(at least, that's what I think).

Tom loves Steffie Sloppysocks
and she loves Pete the Punk,
Pete loves Gretchen Gumhead
and she loves Sam the Skunk.

Sam loves Linda Lemonmouth
and she loves Fred the Flea,
Fred's in love with Jelly Jill
…I wonder who loves me.

• MY FATHER'S VALENTINE •

I'm working on a valentine,
my very special own design,
a heart to give my dad tonight
(it's quite a chore to get it right).

The first time that I cut it out,
one side was thin, the other stout,
and so I tried to fix it, but
I made an error when I cut.

I wasn't careful (though I tried),
and overcut the other side,
but one more snip should do it, then
whoops! I cut too much again.

A snip off here, a snip off there,
and maybe just another hair,
it's finally done, but understand
it's somewhat smaller than I'd planned.

It's not much bigger than a bean,
the tiniest heart I've ever seen,
I guess I'll give it to him now…
I bet he likes it anyhow.

• I ONLY GOT ONE VALENTINE •

I only got one valentine,
and *that* was signed

LOVE,
FRANKENSTEIN

JACK PRELUTSKY was born and raised in New York City, but now makes his home in Albuquerque, New Mexico. He has been entertaining young readers for years with his funny and original books of poems, including *The Sheriff of Rottenshot, Rolling Harvey Down the Hill,* and three ALA Notable books: *The Queen of Eene, The Snopp on the Sidewalk,* and *Nightmares,* a chilling collection of monster poems. He has also translated several books of German and Swedish verse, including *The Wild Baby* and *The Wild Baby Goes to Sea* by Barbro Lindgren.

YOSSI ABOLAFIA was born in Tiberias, Israel. As an animation director he has worked in Israel, Canada, and the United States. For Greenwillow he has illustrated *Harry's Visit* by Barbara Ann Porte and *Buffy and Albert* by Charlotte Pomerantz.